Ink: A Writing Life

Ink: A Writing Life

Stephanie Grace Whitson

Published by Story Architect, 52 Mission Circle, Suite 122, PMB 170, Santa Rosa, CA 95409-5370

The author is represented by Books & Such Literary Agency, Inc., 5926 Sunhawk Drive, Santa Rosa, CA 95409.
www.booksandsuch.com

I've not been called to laud the fame
Of prophets, priests, or kings,
But oh, the lessons I have learned
Observing simple things.

Foreword
How It All Began

Words were important to me back at my beginning—before even my earliest conscious memories. I don't remember the game my older siblings used to play, but my mother (may she rest in peace) used to tell me how they made a game of teaching me new words—a new word every day when they got home from school. As a result, when I was about two years old, I didn't call a book a book. I called it a *dictionary.* I doubt I pronounced it correctly, but my siblings found it immensely entertaining to watch the expression on strangers' faces when I used the big words they'd taught me.

Mother was a word person, too. Robbed of the opportunity to go to high school by a cruel father who said, "I didn't need it and you don't either" (in spite of the fact a teacher had offered to house, feed, and clothe a promising student), my mother educated herself by reading. I grew up in a house where books were important. One of my earliest memories is Mother reading *Pinocchio* aloud to me when I was in bed suffering from what she called *scarlatina*. Mother loved poetry, and I cherish her copy of the *Best Loved Poems of the American People* because of the notations about this or that poem—the name of a dear friend or a comment in agreement with a sentiment. I also cherish a poem she authored on the occasion of my second birthday and another she sent me when my husband and I purchased our first home. Mother's set of Elsie Dinsmore novels are now in the possession of the third generation of descendants who love words—her granddaughter (currently raising her own crop of word people).

My father didn't have the opportunity for what he called "book learning," either. Daddy was in the eighth grade when his father left their farm in southern Illinois, abandoning his wife and four children. Daddy had to drop out of school and go home to plow behind a mule in a largely unsuccessful attempt to grow a crop that would feed the family. I remember him telling stories of lard sandwiches and hand-me-down coats that were several sizes too large. He suffered malnutrition so severe that a case of rickets left him with a malformed rib cage. But Daddy read, too. His favorite novel was Charles Sheldon's *In His Steps*. His Bible was well worn: he underlined favorite passages and jotted notes in the margins. A poem he wrote about truck driving at Christmas was published in a trade magazine.

My parents were careful to teach me the proper names of the things in our world. A tree was an oak, a sugar maple, a sweet gum, a gingko. The flowering bushes in the yard were forsythia, mock orange, flowering quince, viburnum, cardinal bush. Mother's flowers? Wabash and cameo iris, gallardia, shasta daisies, and bleeding hearts—the latter because they were her mother's favorite. As an adult traveling to do historical research or attend writing events, I've annoyed many a cab driver asking for the name of a blooming tree or a beautiful hedge in a city I was visiting. They never seem to know. They aren't word people.

My parents' generation didn't talk about s-e-x. In fact, Mother once told me that Mamo (Daddy's mother) would leave the room if someone said the word *pregnant* in her presence. But Mother believed in giving her children words. When I asked questions about private things, they were answered matter-of-factly. No shame, no blushing, no secrecy. The correct words for human anatomy, bodily functions, and reproductive processes. No nicknames, no silly euphemisms. The right words. I did not at the time realize how unusual that was. I have since come to realize it was all part of the legacy of words given me by my uneducated but well-read parents.

I was "the caboose" in our family. My siblings were 9, 11, and 13 when I was born. That's me in my sister's arms in 1952. I was the flower girl in her wedding when I was only five years old. None of my parents' friends had children my age, and so I grew up in the company of adults. I was bright but socially awkward around kids my age—on the rare occasion I was around other kids outside of school. Books provided friends, new worlds, and escape. I spent countless hours reading, cradled by a perfectly shaped limb of a mulberry tree in our backyard in East St. Louis, Illinois. Walter Farley (*The Black Stallion*) and Marguerite O'Hara (*Thunderhead, Green Grass of Wyoming*) carried me to new worlds. My parents invested in a set of classics. I met Robinson Crusoe and Robin Hood. As I grew, page counts increased. I read *Gone with the Wind* five times. Yes, *five*.

My first foray into creative writing involved a fascination with the poetry of Robert Frost. Mrs. Younghouse, my sixth-grade teacher at Edgemont Elementary School in East St. Louis, Illinois, had her students making scrapbooks about poet Robert Frost. Pardon the bad pun, but the words to Frost's "Stopping by Woods on a Snowy Evening" struck a chord with me, so I set them to music. I also loved the writing exercise Mrs. Younghouse introduced that year, setting up a piece of artwork on an easel and asking the class to write something about what they saw. I remember a winter scene and footprints in the snow. I don't know what I wrote, but I loved the wordplay resulting from what I now call a novelist's best friend—an overactive imagination.

Mrs. Virginia Jenkins at Clark Junior High School in East St. Louis, Illinois, taught me the importance of getting it right when it came to words. Frustrated by her English class's seeming indifference to the importance of spelling, she once demanded that we write each word we'd misspelled on a recent test five *hundred* times. Say what you will about the assignment given in anger, I've never since misspelled the word *receive*. Another English teacher at Clark oversaw the publication of a junior high anthology of poems, and two of mine were included.

High school introduced me to new words—in French. As part of the graduating class of 1969, I knew I would want a college degree, and to get into most colleges back then, a student had to have two years of a foreign language in high school. Mine offered only German or French. I knew (where I learned this, I have no idea) that German nouns could be masculine, feminine, or neuter. French nouns were either masculine or feminine. In spite of my German heritage on my mother's side, I opted for French because it sounded easier. As it turned out, it *was* easy. Two excellent French teachers brought art and music and architecture and history alive for me, and I fell in love with a beautiful, beautiful language.

As for instruction in English, I was blessed with Miss Dorothy McMullen for tenth grade English. Miss McMullen was the topic of much conversation outside of the classroom, most of it centered around how long we thought her hair would be if she ever let it down out of that bun so carefully arranged at the back of her head. Miss McMullen of the mysterious hair didn't hesitate to write a big *F* at the top of a paper containing a run-on sentence. Wonderful content and big thoughts aside, grammar mattered, and Miss McMullen had no favorites in that regard. As to the hair question, we learned she could sit on it. She took it down one day, thereby affirming our class status at the top of her list of Favorite Classes I Have Taught.

I attended Southern Illinois University, the Edwardsville campus. By then, I knew I was a word person. I was the weird student who didn't groan when assigned an essay or a term paper or any other bit of writing. I loved it. All of it in every form. I wrote poetry and term papers with delight. My senior year I fell in love with and married a gifted musician. He wrote songs about his Christian faith, and I sometimes contributed lyrics. When we moved away from southern Illinois and embraced Nebraska as our forever home, I committed to letter-writing to keep in touch with family. I also learned that writing about a conflict or a troublesome episode in life or writing *to* a teenager about a matter of discipline offered me the opportunity for self-expression without the kind of emotion that might cloud what was really important—communicating.

My love of words birthed an inspirational gift company when our children were young and a twenty-plus-year life as a published novelist after that. And so it is. I've been a word person for nearly seventy years, and here I am pounding out more words for a book intended to gather up some of the words I deem worth saving, most of them written before I became a published novelist.

From time to time, folks who've heard me give one of the talks I give to church groups based on my life experiences ("A Patchwork Life," "Got Hope?," "How to Help a Grieving Friend," "Women of the Word") have said, "you should write a book about your life." I've always cringed at the idea. Why would anyone care to read about my life? If you have read this far, I guess you are one of the interested. And so I offer these words of my life with a sincere thanks to you for reading them. I hope they make you smile, provide catharsis, encourage your heart, or in some other way I can't imagine give you joy. You, dear reader, have already done all those things for me in countless notes and e-mails and Facebook messages over the years. Thank you for the words you've given me. They mean more than you'll ever know.

Stephanie Grace Whitson
Lincoln, Nebraska

Spring, 2019

Table of Contents

Legacy

. . . thou hast given me the heritage of those that fear thy name.
Psalm 61:5b

My mother, Nora Odel Combs Irvin, was born in 1913. Her mother, Barbara Johanna Heinecke Combs, passed away in 1923. A baby girl born shortly before Barbara's death was given up for adoption, leaving Nora and her older brother, George, at the mercy of a man whose faults shall remain unspoken here. For a while, Mother lived with relatives who made her the scapegoat for their favored only child, also a girl. When Mother was old enough to cook and clean for her father and brother, she was brought home and treated like chattel. Her first job away from home was as a maid for "the wealthiest woman in town," someone Mother always spoke of fondly. Realizing that she'd never be able to afford a home of her own on a maid's salary, Mother left that position and went to work as a presser at a dress factory. She was befriended by a co-worker who introduced her to my father by way of a blind date. They were married in 1938, and while the deep emotional scars from her early life created lifelong challenges for her, Mother was a faithful wife who raised four children, served in her local church, and accomplished more than anyone who knew the details of her early life would ever have expected. She also made the best blackberry cobbler on the planet.

Cecil Grayson Irvin was born on a southern Illinois farm in 1915. When he was in eighth grade, his father abandoned the family. Daddy left school to help ensure the survival of his mother and three siblings. He plowed behind a mule and remembered taking grain to the mill to be ground into flour so his mother could make bread. He also remembered lard sandwiches. And hunger. He was a trucker when he took Mother on that blind date. They married in 1938. The desire to provide a better life for his family led Daddy to Yellow Freight in St. Louis, Missouri, for whom he would work for the rest of his professional life, racking up Million Miler awards for safe driving and serving his fellow drivers by creating a widow's fund to help the families of drivers who lost their lives in traffic accidents. Daddy was gone a lot, but when he was home, he was *home.* He loved fishing with his boys and the St. Louis Cardinals. I cherish memories of attending baseball games with him when I was in junior high school, climbing up to seats in the very top of the stadium, seats awarded for my excellent grades—seats that enabled us to root for a team that would win the World Series in 1964.

My parents passed away in 1996 within six weeks of each other. Their life together was not always "happily ever after," and yet in 58 years of marriage, they modeled the very meaning of the word *commitment.* The legacy of having that word lived out "for better or for worse" continues in my life today.

A Birthday Poem for Stephanie

January 26, 1954
By Mother

This day our blond with hair of gold
will be exactly two years old—
our daughter, little Stephanie,
who never patters anywhere
but what at her the people stare,
beholding her say, say "My, she's sweet."

The day this verse in print appears,
she will have lived two happy years.
Just two swift years of sun and shade,
already countless conquests made.
Must she forget, as grown-ups do,
the time when she was only two?

My second birthday came and went.
Long lost has been that glad event.
But it may be, when I have gone,
That she, grown-up, will come upon
This verse, in which the joy I've told
We had when she was two years old.

Prayer for Drivers at Christmas Time

By Cecil G. Irvin

God give me health and common sense
to drive the way I ought,
To watch the road and follow
all the rules I have been taught.

I will observe the signs that say
to stop, or lower speed,
And when some child appears ahead,
I will take a special heed.

I will be careful at each turn
or motions that I make
And let the other drivers know
the course that I will take.

I will be mindful of the wheel,
the pedal on the floor,
The shift, the mirror, instruments,
The tightness of the door.

I promise to be sober, Lord,
and always drive my best.
Just give me health and common sense,
and I will do the rest.

Faith

Now to Him who is able to do far more abundantly beyond all that we ask or think, according to the power that works within us, to Him be the glory in the church and in Christ Jesus to all generations forever and ever. Amen.

Ephesians 3:20-21 NASB

Unlike my siblings, I have no memory of my parents before they knew Jesus Christ as personal Savior ("For God so loved the world, that he gave his only begotten Son, that whosoever believeth in him should not perish, but have everlasting life." –John 3:16 KJV). We lived right around the corner from Fifteen Street Baptist Church in East St. Louis, Illinois, and if the doors were open, we were there. Daddy was a deacon. Mother taught children's Sunday School and Vacation Bible School and served in the Women's Missionary Society. My older siblings sang in the choir.

When I was nine years old, I went forward after a Sunday evening service and asked to attend the class our pastor, Reverend Leininger, taught for those wishing to be baptized. Reverend Leininger took baptism seriously, and he didn't perform the rite for anyone unless he'd taken them through a few sessions of Bible teaching regarding the gospel. He was known to refuse baptism if he didn't feel comfortable with someone's spiritual understanding of the serious personal commitment they were making to Christ.

While my understanding of the gospel includes the belief that there is a moment in time when a person crosses over from "lost" to "saved," I don't honestly know when that moment in time occurred in my young life. I do know that when I was standing in the baptismal next to Reverend Leininger and he asked me to speak my name aloud, I knew that I was a sinner ("For all have sinned, and come short of the glory of God." –Romans 3:23 KJV) and that only Jesus' death on the cross could cancel my sin debt, pay the wages of death, and close the gap between me and a holy God ("For the wages of sin is death; but the gift of God is eternal life through Jesus Christ our Lord." –Romans 6:23 KJV). I believed in that moment—and probably had believed for a while—that only the blood of Jesus shed on the cross could wash away my sin and enable me to stand forgiven before God and become His child. I remember that when I spoke my name aloud that evening, I was consciously offering myself and my future to God because of what Jesus had done for me on the cross.

My faith wasn't really challenged until I went to college, but during those four years I had many opportunities to decide whether I believed the Bible because I had been taught to believe it or whether I believed it because I personally thought it was true. I went through a time of serious questioning. By God's grace I clung to my simple faith in the message of the Bible.

As an active part of the InterVarsity Christian Fellowship at SIUE, I joined in praying for one of our members' roommates. His name was Bob Whitson. I remember the day in 1973 when Bob first greeted the group of believers gathered in the student union. It was the day after he had made his own personal commitment to Christ. He and I were married later that year. In 1975 he was working as a nursing home administrator when we were transferred from Arlington Heights, Illinois, to Lincoln, Nebraska.

After a summer of visiting many different churches in Lincoln, Bob and I settled in at what was then called Indian Hills Community Church of the Mennonite Brethren. We were drawn there by the young pastor's commitment to teaching the Bible to his congregation. Neither of us had ever heard a preacher who methodically taught through the Bible verse by verse, but we were hungry to learn. Learning God's Word alongside a community of the faithful had a profound and positive impact on our daily lives.

My family has not been spared difficulty. Over the years we've encountered financial stress, serious illness, death (Bob died of cancer in 2001), and more. We've survived by God's grace. Bob died in God's grace. By God's grace I remarried the widowed husband of my best female friend who had died of breast cancer four days after Bob was diagnosed. If I have thrived in this life, it is a testimony to the living and powerful Word of God ("For the word of God is living and active and sharper than any two-edged sword, and piercing as far as the division of soul and spirit, of both joints and marrow, and able to judge the thoughts and intentions of the heart." –Hebrews 4:12 NASB) taught by a faithful servant and lived out in the lives of the community of believers God led me to over forty years ago. I have been blessed to experience what musician and Bible scholar Michael Card calls "joy in the journey," and I believe the promise that God will be faithful to complete the good work He began in me when I was only nine years old.

For I am confident of this very thing, that He who began a good work in you will perfect it until the day of Christ Jesus.
Philippians 1:6 NASB

Devotional Thoughts and Essays

So teach us to number our days, that we
may present to You a heart of wisdom.
Psalm 90:12 NASB

Prisms

Eternal rainbows fixed in a lead-fringed sky soar above the congregation. Most of the pieces are simply cut, their varied hues of purple, gold, and green forming lovely scenarios. At intervals along the glass greenery trimming each scene, flowers bloom, their petals formed by a few simple pieces of translucent glass. At the center of each flower, a prism catches the light in its finely cut depths and flings it onto the walls in brilliant splashes of color. Unlike the pieces of stained glass that would be uninteresting apart from their companion pieces, a prism deserves attention—even hanging alone on a slender thread.

In the Christian walk it is good to be reminded that, just like the prism, we become more significant in the kingdom as we bend ourselves to be cut and polished by the greatest Craftsman of all. As trials cut away at our self-sufficiency, we learn to reflect His will more perfectly. By losing part of our sinful selves, we are changed from a lackluster hunk of glass into a prism that shines for God's glory.

Superwoman Syndrome

[Published in Indian Hills Community Church women's newsletter *A Servant's Heart,* 1980]

The television commercial portrays a woman alternately attired in business suit, house robe, and evening gown. She's singing, "I can bring home the bacon, fry it up in a pan, and never let you forget you're a man." The lyrics espouse a philosophy of womanhood prevalent when it was first aired in the late 1900s, but no less relevant today. For lack of a better term, call it "Superwoman Syndrome." Translated into everyday living, the syndrome promotes the ideology that the only truly fulfilled woman is the one who, while aspiring to become a CEO, also takes an evening class in French, bakes bread from scratch, and has ample time left over for needlepoint and a meaningful family life.

Superwoman Syndrome doesn't just attack women outside the church. Especially in large congregations where there are many women to admire, one can easily begin to aspire to become the best. Keep an immaculate home. Bake from scratch. Become a nutrition expert.

Be continually available to your children. Keep abreast of current events. Teach a Bible study. Learn a new craft every month. Be an exceptional wife. The list goes on and keeping one can make finding a "gentle and quiet spirit" difficult if not impossible. At its worst, a list like that can lead to recurrent depression stemming from a continual feeling of failure.

One of the most freeing biblical concepts I know is that God meets us where we are and uses the talents He bestowed to polish us so that we sparkle just as *He* desires. The different spiritual gifts He endows indicate that variety is inherent in God's ideal for each woman. We are not intended to become a carbon copy of some celestial Superwoman. Just as every woman does not have the same spiritual gift, so every woman will not be the same in her everyday life. All do *not* bake bread from scratch. All do *not* give only handmade Christmas gifts. All do *not* make their own clothes. All do *not* garden.

As unique creations of our sovereign Lord, we women need to praise God for His bestowal of our individual abilities and leave Superwoman Syndrome where it belongs—in the world, not the church.

Kofax

Were there a Salvation Army for felines, Kofax would be one of their most hopeless derelicts. She has no dignity, no self-respect, and no beauty. To gaze upon her is to see all the undesirable traits of a cat. Her tail is a scrawny yellow string, her body persistently thin, her coat without luster—an attempt at stripes failing miserably somewhere along the rib cage.

Her expression is one of continual apology. Apology for meowing, apology for entering the room, apology for crawling into a lap—apology for existing. Yellow eyes look off in different directions, giving her a lost, out-of-touch look. The mouth turns upward in a silly half-smile. The ears continually twitch in a futile attempt to catch every sound, so as to be prepared for immediate retreat to her sanctuary—a pile of tires. She is without redeeming qualities, save one.

She is mine.

An Empty House

(Published in the *Good News Broadcaster*, November, 1984)

The house across the street is empty. It has been empty for many weeks now. Its owner is hospitalized by the vicious disease of cancer. But this morning at 4:00, his heart gave one last beat—a sigh, a pulse, and then no more. So the house stands empty now, its curtains drawn, its face staring into a world that has one less citizen.

Neighbors have tended the house in its owner's absence. The grass has been mowed, the papers and mail taken in. And now the mail will stop. The paperboy will cross a name off his route.

I have watched that house for a long time. Some time ago, having watched its drapes being drawn and shut against the light of each day, I trembled with fear at the thought of sharing the Gospel with the house's occupant. He was not religious, I'd been told. He was hard to get along with. He had had a hard life. He hated the God who allowed his wife to remain in a nursing home—physically alive but mentally dead. And so, in fear, I waited. Perhaps God would burden someone else to share the Gospel. I had no right to invade his world in this time of trouble.

These thoughts swirled in my mind from day to day as I watched the house and prayed for its occupant—until the burden became so great that I could no longer bear it. I had to tell.

You know without a doubt that this man will go to hell if he dies without Christ. You also know that he <u>*is*</u> *dying, and the end could be soon. How can you wait? How can you be silent? You've built a relationship. You've shown that you care in human ways. Now show that you care in the ultimate sense! Forget your pride, your fear of rejection, whatever else is keeping you away! Go and tell that man about Me before it's too late... before it's too late... before it's too late...."*

And so I went. In fear. In trembling. I smiled. We talked. I shared. He listened. He heard the Good News. And this morning at 4:00 he entered eternity. It breaks my heart to think of the frail body lying in a hospital bed, the stubborn spirit still flashing behind angry eyes, shaking a bony first at the very God who loved him enough to die on a cross.

I have never known anyone well who died and who may be in hell. The news of his death has shattered my day, and as I type these random feelings my tears flow freely. The house across the street is empty. But the grass will keep growing for some new owner who will inherit wild honeysuckle growing over a rotting arbor and strawberries borne on the plants now heavy with blossoms. Through sobs I wonder if the one who planted them also lives on—in eternal life rather than eternal death. The awesomeness of the latter possibility overwhelms me.

And the only comfort I have is that I shared, and he listened. *Oh God, thank You for giving me time to overcome my fears. Thank You for carrying my feet across the street to tell. Thank You that this day I don't have to deal with the guilt that I had the message of eternal life but kept it to myself. It still hurts terribly, Lord, to think he may not have believed. But at least he heard.*

The house across the street is empty. But other occupants will come. And through my tears I look ahead to the new neighbors, and I pray for them even now—and for myself, that once again I will not be silent.

A Broken Pitcher

[Published in 1986 by *The Upper Room Daily Devotional Guide*]

I carefully collect each broken piece of the old pitcher. I had held it securely in hand seconds before, washing off the dust. Just an old pitcher. *But I like it so much.* Its bronze and blue flowers on a cream-colored background had caught my eye at an auction years ago, thinking it would look so nice in my soon-to-be-blue kitchen. I bought the pitcher, delighted that no one else appreciated its colors and shape as much as I.

I enjoy sorting the china puzzle, and I whisper a praise for "super-glue." My colorful accent piece will be salvaged with only a few more creases on its surface. But why do I bother? It isn't worth much, this pitcher. Just one more thing to dust. Why do I bother? Because I like it very much. It pleases me to salvage it because I like it—not because it has any monetary value, but just because it is.

As I piece together my broken pitcher, it reminds me of God who mends broken things. Eternal Love takes broken lives and restores their original beauty. God takes the time to mend what others might throw away, not because they are valued in the marketplace but because God loves them.

Peer Pressure or Pride?

[Published in Indian Hills Community Church women's newsletter *A Servant's Heart,* 1982]

The phone rang and the caller and I inched our way into a discussion that involved an uncomfortable area for us both. The caller had a need for prayer support as she faced the challenge of a new conviction to stop smoking. Her need was real. My promise to lend prayer support was sincere. But we both felt uncomfortable talking about *the problem*.

Why is it that believers often feel reluctant to share concerns that are of such a personal nature? True, we cannot—and should not—always share every need with those outside our family. That fact, however, should not keep us from obeying the mandate to "bear one another's burdens" (Gal. 6:2 NASB).

As my caller and I grappled together with our tentative hold on heart-to-heart sharing, there seemed to be two things interfering with the attempt. First, there was *peer pressure*, which can play a subtle role in a church that emphasizes knowledge of the Word and spiritual maturity. In such an environment it is easy for any Christian to feel overwhelmed by the amount of Bible knowledge and apparent spiritual maturity surrounding him/her. In our zeal to grow in the Word, we may give one another the mistaken impression that we "have it all together," that we have conquered the flesh and live in a world of spiritual maturity where "common" sins of the world are not a problem. While the pressure to conform to Christ is desirable, it becomes twisted when it makes us afraid to share the reality of the Christian walk with one another.

That leads to the second thing that can interfere with the proper bearing of one another's burdens. If I respond in *pride* to the peer pressure of a church that emphasizes Christian maturity, I will not want others to know that I have a particular problem. Wanting other believers to think that I, too, am "mature," I will be afraid to admit that smoking or fear of witnessing or lack of a daily time in the Word is a constant problem for me.

Churches where believers are afraid to share one another's burdens can easily become cold entities where the life of Christ is stifled. If no problems are shared and no prayers are offered up on behalf of others, then no joy of victory can be experienced as a body. Satan robs us of the joy of the battle, which is victory over ourselves and thus, over him.

The phone call ended with a measure of success. I have a new name on my prayer list. My friend knows that someone who also has problems and failures is supporting her in prayer as she fights her own personal battle with self-control. Both of us are looking forward to the enjoyment of mutual celebration when the battle is won. We have learned that peer pressure and pride must be overcome before the Body of Christ is made alive to us in its fullest sense. From my friend's courage in "breaking the ice," I hope to have learned that just as Christ died for me while I was yet a sinner, so I can live with others who are his, for we are *all* sinners, regardless of our level of maturity.

Prayer

[Published in Indian Hills Community Church women's newsletter *A Servant's Heart,* 1982]

The first thing I must state on the subject prayer is that I do not understand how it works. How can the totally sovereign God who has preordained all of history answer my prayers? I don't know. But He does.

The second thing I can state on the topic of prayer is that after twenty-one years as a believer, I have not yet mastered how to do it. A well-known hymn says, "the pure delight of a single hour that before Thy throne I spend; When I kneel in prayer and with Thee, my God, I commune as friend with Friend." It is very convicting to ponder those words. I have spent many uninterrupted hours sewing, reading, talking on the phone, writing and the like. But I do not remember once talking with God for a similar period. I have never experienced the "pure delight" of an hour before the throne. That admission shames me.

Perhaps one reason for my lack of prayer experience is that 20th century life is very fragmented. Women sew while watching television, listen to tapes while doing dishes, and manage to feel guilty if they stop for even fifteen minutes of quiet, uninterrupted thought. Growing up in this type of world discourages the daily habit of serious prayer. It's much simpler to fulfill 1 Thessalonians 5:17 ("Pray without ceasing") by posting a prayer list over the kitchen sink and flinging sentence fragments heavenward as the day goes by than it is to commit oneself to an extended period of prayer. There is, of course, nothing wrong with brief prayers. But they should never totally supplant the type of prayer reflected in Acts 12 when the saints prayed for an extended period for the imprisoned Peter.

I began a new prayer list today, and in less than five minutes I had compiled enough items to easily occupy on hour of prayer: my husband, my aunt who is dying of cancer, the elders at church as they make decisions, the 1982 evangelistic outreach, my sister who is caring for her infant granddaughter while the single mother works, a friend with a special problem, myself as I take care of our second child, and the future of our 2-½-year-old daughter.

I have the privilege of approaching the throne of the Lord of the universe on behalf of "the beloved." Why don't I? The answers are myriad, but they can be well summarized by putting one other item at the head of my new prayer list: "Lord, change *me*." That item alone is good for a few thousand hours before the throne. Beginning today.

Parenting

[Published in Indian Hills Community Church women's newsletter *A Servant's Heart*, 1982]

"Behold, children are a gift of the Lord" (Ps. 127:3 NASB). It is a modern tragedy that believers must often be *reminded* of God's perspective on parenthood. Attitudes toward family living have changed dramatically in recent years. Only a generation ago it was accepted that marriage resulted in children. Today couples have nearly complete control over when—or if—they will have children.

With the combined pressures of inflation and materialism challenging the young family, couples may find it difficult to list many pros on an inventory of reasons for or against parenting. Even so, Solomon's belief that "children are a gift of the Lord" is still true. Young couples are often ignorant of one aspect of the gift. Marvelous refinement can take place in their own lives when they embark upon the journey into 2:00 a.m. feedings and diapers.

Trusting is the first lesson I recall learning in a new dimension as a result of parenting. Spending the night by my infant daughter's bassinet as she battled a respiratory infection, I felt utterly helpless. I was humbled by my lack of trust and then challenged to renew my faith. It was a graphic lesson because it was taught through a beloved child.

I often wonder how God would teach me **patience** and **self-control** if it were not for the screaming child who simply "would not stop no matter what I tried" or the defiant toddler who stood planted firmly to the floor and stated, "No I NOT" when requested to perform a simple task.

Earnest prayer becomes a fresh reality for parents who send their children off to a secular school, knowing they will be inundated with unbiblical principles and faced with teachers who discount religion as foolishness.

To those childless young women questioning the place of children in their lives: be encouraged to try the unchartered waters of parenting. There are times when I learn something of God through my daughter, and I wonder how He would have taught me had I remained childless. True, the lessons often come through 2:00 a.m. feedings or other "general inconveniences" of parenting. But the blessing of those less-than-blessed moments is in knowing that God uses them to refine me. Even 2:00 a.m. feedings can encourage a mother's spiritual growth. The Psalmist says so. "My eyes anticipate the night watches, that I may meditate on Your word" (Ps. 119:148 NASB).

When the Kids are Grown

[Published in Indian Hills Community Church women's newsletter *A Servant's Heart*, 1981]

A recent letter from my sister reads, "Beginning this week I will spend Wednesdays with a friend who is a terminal cancer patient. I will need God's grace for it, because her cancer is not only in the liver but also an open ulcer at site of a previous mastectomy... doctors say 'no hope,' and her family wants her at home. Ladies at church will take turns so she is never alone until she is healed either here temporarily or permanently at home with Jesus...." I have known for years that my sister is a loving woman of God. The purpose of this editorial, however, is not to praise her, but rather to consider the quality of servanthood she exhibits.

All believers are responsible to serve, "for we are His workmanship, created in Christ Jesus for good works..." (Eph. 2:10 NASB). The home is one realm of service chosen by many young mothers who discipline themselves to unglamorous roles as servants-at-home. However, once the last diaper is changed or the last feet trot away to school, many of these women enter the professional world. Such a decision necessitates readjusting priorities. Unfortunately, the result is often a diminished availability for service in the Body of Christ. At forty, having raised five children, my sister could have breathed a sigh of relief and pursued another career. Instead, she chose to remain at home, and that choice resulted in her being available to serve a Christian sister in desperate need.

Not all Christian women have the privilege of deciding to remain at home once their children are grown. But some who do may exchange aprons for briefcases before considering an alternative. If more Christian women would expand their sphere of service to the church family, countless needs could be met. The results of such self-sacrifice could include harried young mothers given an afternoon away from their children one afternoon a week, nursing home patients cheered by regular visits, and discouraged believers encouraged by servants with time to listen.

Servanthood. No well-known periodical is likely to feature it. No earthly employer gives raises for it. But the King of Kings rewards it. "What will I do when the children are grown?" Remember several women who chose to be available to a friend with terminal cancer. Then consider deciding to "go and do likewise."

Serving or Being Served?

[Published in Indian Hills Community Church women's newsletter *A Servant's Heart*, 1981]

From its inception our newsletter has been intended to encourage an attitude of service among Christian women. In order for Christian women to serve, however, there must be someone willing to be served. Twentieth century mores do not encourage women to acknowledge less than total adequacy, and since accepting help from others means one is not totally self-sufficient, it can be difficult for us to admit needs. Unfortunately, this can result in an inability to be on the receiving end of someone else's serving the Lord. We can even become guilty of a reverse sort of pride that prohibits our admitting a need for help, be that spiritual counseling, prayer, or material assistance. "Thank you for offering, but I can manage" may be voiced too often.

God has used two special couples with the gift of giving to teach me to accept the service of theirs in the material sphere. One couple insists that I use their second car during the day whenever I need it. The other gives away material possessions so gleefully that it puts my own selfishness to shame. I have accepted both couples' help but not without some difficult swallowing of the words "thank you, but no."

An attitude of nonacceptance makes it very difficult, if not impossible, for friends to exercise their spiritual gifts. Caught up in our need to display spiritual maturity, we become afraid to admit our needs in any area, thus the spiritual gifts of others are not exercised as much as they could be.

In the area of material sharing there is often the compulsion to "keep even" with our brothers and sisters in Christ. As the spectre of some imaginary celestial scoreboard flashes our "points," we try to out-give those who have the gift of giving and outdo those with a special knack for hospitality. While it is true that we should seek to outdo one another in love and good deeds, keeping score can sometimes be an unhealthy barrier to the free exercise of our love for one another. Let's learn to allow other believers to serve the Lord they love in their special way—even when that means we must humble ourselves and cry, "Help!" The result should be a local body "...fitted and held together by what every joint supplies, according to the proper working of each individual part" and "the growth of the body for the building up of itself in love" (Ephesians 4:16 NASB).

Spoon-feeding?

[Published in Indian Hills Community Church women's newsletter *A Servant's Heart,* 1981]

The recent demise of a local radio station devoted to religious programming left a void in the life of this writer. Unable to tune in KGBI programming from Omaha, I was forced to withdraw from Christian radio "cold turkey." No longer would John MacArthur, Jr., exhort me to more biblical Christian living. No longer would I laugh at a Hendricks' anecdote or cry with a Dobson counselee. It was a shock. My daily spiritual warfare was now my sole responsibility.

Then something happened. With no one to feed me, it appeared I would have to feed myself. For the first time in my twenty years as a believer, daily Bible reading became a habit.

With no one to exhort me to prayer, I would have to pray alone. I began to converse with God throughout the day in sentence requests ("Please, Lord, help me keep my sense of humor" as the baby spewed oatmeal all over the new wallpaper) and praises, ("Thank you, Lord, for the oatmeal.")

With no Christian radio companions to share my kitchen, I had to reach out for more creative kinds of communication. Our being a one-car family precluded weekday involvement in a women's Bible study. I found myself more faithful in correspondence, more attuned to others' needs, more appreciative of their gifts.

The experience has caused me to question the place of Christian radio in the lives of full-time homemakers. Are we overly dependent upon chapels of the air for our spiritual well-being? Have we come to rely too much on spoon-feeding and too little on our own study? Do we miss opportunities to quiet meditation or conversation with the Lord because our world is filled with background music?

Of course not all women will answer these questions identically, but they do merit consideration. While we thank God for His use of the electric church, we must not allow it to replace our own study of the Bible. Radio broadcasters may teach us *about* prayer, but they can also usurp quiet moments when we could pray.

If we are to fight the good fight against the roaring lions of this anti-biblical "do your own thing, you've come a long way, baby" society, we must mature in Christ. Maturity is effected as we study. Christian radio and tapes are a blessing, but may we never forget that our spiritual growth depends on personal time in the Word and communion with God. The issue is one of finding the proper balance in our diet of spiritual food.

Chain Reaction

[Published in the Indian Hills Community Church women's newsletter *A Servant's Heart*, 1988]

Somewhere at the beginning of this day there *was* a plan. I meant to help Zachary, my five-year-old son, clean his room. He needed a mirror in his room, so I reasoned we would simply trade his dresser (no mirror) for his sister's (she has three mirrors in her room). It seemed a reasonable task for a college graduate. But somewhere between the slime-covered aquarium and the overstuffed dresser drawers, the plan went awry.

Trading dressers means unloading and sorting an array of shorts, blouses, underwear, marbles, and pipe-cleaners (children's dresser drawers harbor interesting collections). As long as we're moving the dressers, we might as well clean the floors underneath and behind them, right? The dust balls behind Zach's dresser yield two barrettes, five paper clips, a broken car, the missing wheel from his favorite Jeep, and a dead fish. So we pause for a fish funeral—conducted hastily over the toilet bowl burial site.

NOW we can trade dressers. No, not quite. Zach's old dresser has been the table for his aquarium. Since the new dresser will have a mirror for him to stand in front of to comb his hair and so on, we need to find a new table for the aquarium. We scour the house and find a sturdy table in the basement—laden with scraps of wood, a box of tools, and a stereo speaker awaiting repair. We leave the wood, tools, and speaker to be put away later, scrub the table, and tote it up two flights of stairs. It's too high and too unstable for the aquarium.

Not to worry, the table supporting the window fan will be perfect! Except then what do we use for the window fan? Oh, yeah ... that mahogany table in the dining room will work. Except that we'll have to find a new place for the plant that's sitting on it.

The plant gets moved to the TV in the family room (where it eventually expires from lack of light). The mahogany table takes on the window fan, but not before I haul the twenty-pound fan into the tub for a thorough cleaning.

There! The fan is clean. I'll scour the tub later. We set up the fan on the table from the dining room and take the fan table to Zach's room for his aquarium, which sloshes water onto the carpet as I move it from dresser-top to table. Not to worry, the bath towels need washing anyway, so I'll just blot up the water and launder the towels later.

Finally! Zach's room looks great. New dresser and mirror in place, toys put away, bed made. My elation lasts about ten seconds. Brooke's room is now a mess, with her new dresser awaiting organization. I can hardly walk through the upstairs hall because of the pile of fish-smelling towels, the box of miscellany from Zach's room to be sorted, and the vacuum cleaner. There's an empty spot in the dining room where once stood a lovely mahogany table. Bob's work area in the basement is a disaster with scrap lumber and tools from the originally borrowed table waiting to be put somewhere. The tub is a greasy mess from cleaning the fan. Bob is due home from work in ten minutes. I'm exhausted, and what do I have to show for the day's work? Zachary's room looks great. WHO CARES?

What have I been *doing* all day? Nobody told me there would be days like this as I sat in my French literature class at the university. No one prepared me for *this* part of homemaking.

I survey the disaster and God pours out grace. Instead of hanging my head and having a good cry, I laugh. A hard day's work that barely shows. A husband due home in ten minutes to a hall he can hardly navigate and a tired wife... but also a rare sight—a neat five-year-old boy's room. Somewhere in here there's a lesson, Lord. Help me to find it. But first, let's just have a good laugh together!

The First Christmas Without Dad

[Originally published in *God Rest Ye Grumpy Scroogeymen: New Traditions for Comfort and Joy at Christmas,* by Laura Jensen Walker and Michael K. Walker, 2003

Subsequently published in *Christmas Moments: 50 Inspirational Stories of the True Meaning of Christmas,* compiled and edited by Yvonne Lehman, 2014]

Bob and I took care to establish traditions that would ensure that Christmas was the best holiday of the year for our family. One of the more unusual of those traditions was that someone in our family always got a box of dirt. Never mind the significance. It was just part of what it meant to be a Whitson. But as my four children (ages twenty-one, eighteen, fifteen, and twelve) and I faced Christmas 2001, no one cared about the box of dirt. Dad had died of cancer the previous February.

Grief is a strange journey. Sometimes it leads us straight at the thing we dread, and we face it down.

Sometimes we need to take a detour to avoid the dreaded thing until we are stronger. As Christmas approached, I felt we all needed the detour. A phone call provided it, but it took me a few days to embrace it.

A dear niece had been living in Geneva, Switzerland, for two years. Was there any way the children and I could spend Christmas with her?

No, I didn't think so.

Maybe.

I would get back to her.

At the last minute, I asked something absurd. If we came to Geneva, did she think we might also be able to spend a few days in Paris? I'd lived in France when I was in college, and I had always longed to return.

Laura didn't hesitate. Of course! It would be great fun. Just let her know. She'd see what she could do about finding hotel deals.

I hung up and contemplated the obstacles. My two oldest children had jobs. They wouldn't be able to get away. They were both in love. They wouldn't want to leave for a week at Christmas.

And the money. Oh, the money.

As it turned out, the airfare was miraculously cheap. The two oldest children wanted to go. Their bosses let them off. My financial advisor approved: Bob would approve, he said. I thought he was probably right. And so, on Christmas Eve of 2001, instead of crying our way through the usual, we were on our way to Geneva. On Christmas Day instead of stumbling into the Daddy-less living room and pretending to enjoy opening presents, we were fighting jet lag, walking the medieval streets of Geneva, and eating dinner with an international group of Laura's friends from Switzerland, Sweden, and England. My Midwestern children loved it.

The day after Christmas we boarded the TGV and sped to Paris. I speak French and I adore Paris. This part of my life predated my falling in love with their father. There were no sad memories to confront here. I couldn't wait to share Paris with my children. Would they "get it"?

Standing before Notre Dame Cathedral, my son asked, "When did you say they built that?"

"In the 1200s."

He stepped closer to the doors, staring up and up and up at the myriad stone carvings.

Wow.

One night we rode the metro, emerging along the Seine, admiring a particularly beautiful bridge and watching an excursion boat make its way up the river before advancing beyond the row of trees shading the walkway. The Eiffel Tower loomed above us in the night, its ironwork glowing bronze in the lights.

Wow.

On another night we read the sign mounted on a tall iron fence not too far from our hotel near the Sorbonne and discovered we'd been casually walking past the third-century ruins of a Roman bath. *Roman.* As in Julius Caesar and togas.

Wow.

We grabbed floor plans of the Louvre one day just before it closed, and that evening in our hotel room I told the children to look it over and mark the three things they most wanted to see. I wanted them to see less and appreciate more—to remember more than a maze of marbled halls.

The next morning at the museum, I watched my children watch. What would they really see? It turned out to be the Greek/Roman/Italian sculpture. My children were in awe. Their mother was delighted. They were getting it... they really were getting it.

In those four days, we probably walked five miles a day. We didn't see the Musée d'Orsay or go up the Eiffel Tower or ride on an excursion boat or eat at a fancy restaurant or do any number of a zillion things tourists usually go to Paris to see and do. We did, however, climb the towers of Notre Dame and see the gargoyles. We walked the streets of Little Athens and marveled over the array of foods. We shopped at the century old La Samaritaine department store. We ate mussels and crepes and lychees, discovered Nutella, and marveled at the smallness of the cars and the beauty of the roses at a flower market. We made mistakes and got lost.

I don't imagine I'll ever spend Christmas in Paris again. But in 2001 traveling far, far away from home helped one heartbroken family detour around a monster named Grief. We spent our first Christmas without Dad in the City of Lights. Of course, Dad spent the day with the One who said, "Let there be light." But we did all right, too, because we came home knowing that we were going to be all right. We would return to the beloved traditions the next Christmas, and we would smile through our tears when the lucky recipient opened that box of dirt.

Roses

[Originally published in Indian Hills Community Church women's newsletter *A Servant's Heart,* 1981]

Pre-children, my husband and I joined forces and created flower beds in our small yard that once merited inclusion on the annual city Garden Club tour. This essay was inspired by the two dozen hybrid tea roses that formed part of that garden.

Spring never lasts long enough in Nebraska. Winter snow has barely melted and the tulips have just finished blooming, when the sun relentlessly hurls us into summer's heat. But enduring heat is not without its rewards, among them the radiant colors in our flower beds. They bloom profusely, each lending its hue to the rainbow of color that wraps around our yard.

The roses! Such grand flowers! One, completely open, bares its heart to the world. Its translucent ivory petals are laced with tinges of pink—the shade of baby cheeks after a good cry. Another bloom contributes a bold splash of red to the garden. Its petals curl back at the edges like the painted lips of a mischievous girl's smile. The palest rose peeks shyly from behind a verdant leaf. Presently hiding its golden petals, it will open later when the other roses are nearly finished, thereby winning admiration without having to compete. Two deep pink roses embrace the light with ruddy-complexioned petals as if to say, "Look at us!"

The roses are like Christians I know—some bold, others shy. Some easily share their emotions while others hold back. And just as I look at roses and see only beauty, overlooking minor flaws in single petals, forgetting the thorns that prick my fingers, so God looks at His bouquet of children—each one created for his own place, each one lovely, each one playing a vital role in the beauty of the bouquet. It is the contrast of colors, the difference in form, the variety of bloom, that create beauty.

May we as Christians remember that in God's plan there is a place for every bloom. Just as we pluck flowers from the garden, so does God sovereignly choose personalities to be His own—each one in the Body of Christ for a specific service, each one contributing to the exquisite beauty of His Bride, the Church.

The Pitcher

Of all the pitchers in my modest collection, my favorite is a cracked warrior of days gone by. It is almost white … but not quite. The glazed finish that once shone brightly in some store window is now dulled with time. Embellished by fringes of brown, a checkerboard pattern of cracks scatters across its finish. On one side there is the faded imprint of flowers faintly colored in pink and blue. The scalloped lip of the pitcher dips at one edge, forming a shallow spout. A gracefully curved handle is attached to the body, which widens as it nears the base, giving it the form of a dowager who, having raised her brood of youngsters, settles down to enjoy old age without the slightest worry concerning her widening figure.

The charm of the pitcher lies in the character etched into its finish over the years. The fine web of cracks gives evidence of repeated use. The faded bouquet imprinted on its side betrays countless washings. The pitcher has grown beautiful, not by being set upon a shelf in some china cabinet, but by being taken down and used … and used … and used. The finish has worn, the flowers have faded, and the pitcher has become beautiful, like a grandmother's face creased from years of laughing.

Like pitchers, we Christians are made to be used. God bestows His gifts to each of His vessels that they might enrich the lives of others. And with years of service, as youth fades, we come beautiful, not because we have been saved high on a shelf where we cannot be marred, but because we have been used, emptied, and scrubbed clean, over and over again. That is, after all, what a pitcher is for.

Empty House

An exercise from one of only two writing classes I've ever taken, one in journalism and one in creative writing. I include it here because I think it foreshadows my fascination with abandoned, old farmhouses and the people who lived there.

How many people drive by now without a glance! I am old. Useless. Decrepit. Run down. Those words are so ugly—but then, I am ugly now. Years ago, when Michael allowed me to shelter his family, I was something to be noticed! No one drove by then without looking and wishing I were theirs. The lane was cobblestone, and the trees arched over it, cool and inviting to the carriages that passed. Now, all that comes up the lane is the racoon family that lives in that hollow log over the creek. They scamper across my face at night and screech at me, reminding me I am useless.

Some children came by once on their way to school. They talked very quietly, and I liked them. Especially when John (he was about fourteen years old) told his friend, Mary, that I had been beautiful once. He told her about the fresh whitewash and my hand-wrought shutters. But Mary screeched and said she was afraid a snake would come crawling out at her. So John shrugged his shoulders and they left. They haven't been back for years. They've forgotten me—and Michael.

Josef's First Chance to See

He cradled it in gnarled hands as if it were a living, breathing thing and inhaled softly, shallowly—fearing that filling his lungs would shatter the dream. It was still there! The smell of leather and new print filled his nostrils as he brought it slowly to his cheek, rubbing across the bristly chin, holding it close. Finally, it was opened and a ragged fingernail searched through the pages, caressing the text. *There! There it was!* What his heart had known for so long, it now saw for the first time: "for God so loved the world . . . ." The weathered cheeks grew wet with the joy of reading.

It was dawn before he closed the Book. Then, cradling it in his hands again, he nestled it in a niche beneath a rotted stair. It would be safe there. No one would find it.

Poems

Pleasant words are a honeycomb, sweet
to the soul and healing to the bones.
Proverbs 16:23 NASB

Cocoons

A lifeless shell (to earthly eyes)
Can open, freeing its surprise
To dance on a garden leaf.

Gossamer wings gently hesitate
To fly. And then, as wind abates,
It flutters toward the sky.

Out of sight, it yet exists,
And, dancing on, its wings persist
To unseen garden leaves.

No less alive, though out of sight,
It testifies to each man's plight;
A common destiny.

For each of us must leave behind
A lifeless shell. And earthly-minded
Men can think, "life's done."

It isn't true. Although unseen
We flutter on to gardens green
With joy, alive in Christ.

Alive in Christ, Whose dead cocoon,
Though buried in a garden tomb
Arose to give new life.

Here's hope for all in facing death:
A lifeless shell (to earthly eyes)
Precedes the birth of butterflies.

My Daughter

She's at it again, Lord.
Pushing, shoving, screeching to get by me
and to that table
Where she'll dump pencils,
paper,
books,
and telephone
onto the floor
with squeals of delight.
And I need to get the house cleaned!
We've got company coming for dinner.
Bob's due home any minute.
My hair's a wreck.
Toys are strewn all over the floor.
But Brooke doesn't want those toys.
She wants the pencils, paper, books, and telephone.

I am so like her, Lord.
You give me so much.
Within easy reach are promises,
blessings,
abundant life.
But I push and shove and screech
to get by You
to some other thing
And end up dumping contentment,
gentle, quiet spirit

and peace of mind
onto life's floor.
Help me now, Lord
to pick up Brooke and laugh
instead of tensing up.
Then teach me, Lord,
to be grown up when you say "no" to me,
to see the things as they truly are—just *things*—
to accept contentment as Your gift.
Amen.

A Lesson Too Late

[Published in *A Servant's Heart*, 1988 and *Virtue: The Christian Magazine for Women*, 1990]

Had I known how quickly they would grow,
I would have cherished the moments more.
Those still, dark hours of night
When there was only me
    and the smallest cheek to touch.
I would have marveled more at the utter satin-softness
    and grumbled less about the lost sleep.

Had I known how quickly they would grow,
We would have rocked and cuddled close
    long after sleep returned
To close those infant eyes.
I would have hummed more tunes
    into the hush of night.

But nights grew long, and I soon lost
The joy of my night watch.
I longed for my own pillow, then,
And hastily rocked, put back to bed.

And now they are gone—those quiet nights
While Brooke, or Zach, or Shannon
    lay in my arms, holding tight
To my robe, lest I leave.

Now Brooke is grown—and Zach too busy being "stwong"
　　To cuddle much.
And Shannon learns to crawl away
And sleeps the night. "At last!" I think.
So uninterrupted nights return and
　　I'm amazed to learn
That I shed tears for those quiet times,
　　forever gone,
Of nuzzling and baby grunts and sighs.

My infant days are over now—
　　a new season of life unfolds.
But I would have cherished those nights
　　much more—
Had I known.

The poem that follows once adorned a bear named Nina Patch, a gift product sold by Mulberry Lane, the pattern design company begun by me and my best friend in the 1990s. My mother was a quilter. My father quilted, too. But I didn't learn to love quilts and quilting until, as a young mother, I gathered with new friends to complete a project I'd begun as a teenager and never finished. The friendships formed around that quilting frame have endured. I developed a passionate interest in antique quilts, took classes in dating textiles, started the pattern design company, and bought and sold old quilts and antique textiles. As of the publication of this writing memoir, I volunteer at the International Quilt Study Center and Museum in my home town, belong to the American Quilt Study Group, and enjoy incorporating quilts and quilting into my historical fiction. I guess you could say I have a case of "patchwork fever."

Patchwork Fever

There is fabric in the closet,
    and it migrates down the hall
To the basket by my sewing chair,
    then on the floor it falls.
The remnants of my projects
    hide beneath the time-worn couch
With dust bunnies and lost quilting books
    that I forgot about.
Oh, I know that in my lifetime
    I will never see complete
All the projects that I've started—
    but for fun it can't be beat.
For I love to sort my fabrics
    and I love to spread them out
Into patchwork plans and patterns—
    that's what quilting's all about.
Only quilters understand it,
    for they suffer from it, too.
Patchwork Fever is contagious,
    so BEWARE—it might catch you!

Broken

When our plans yield only failure,
  when our dreams have nearly died,
We can run to Christ, and in His cross
  our sorrows He will hide.
From our brokenness the Lord can stitch
  a quilt of golden threads,
Covering failures in our lives
  with His own righteousness.
He transforms life's broken fragments
  into something fine and true.
Keeping every blessed promise,
  He will give a life that's new.

Da Bears

Therefore encourage one another and build up on another, just as you also are doing.
I Thessalonians 5:14 NASB

A Little Background

When we began homeschooling our children, we didn't realize what we were getting into. Our curriculum virtually required that we begin a cottage industry to teach our children practical math and other skills best learned with a hands-on approach. In 1989, we began with an in-home boutique during the holiday season where we sold hand-crafted gift items. The following year, we added craft shows. We'd moved to an acreage by then, and so we became involved in a local farmer's market. The children and I gardened and baked in the summer, and we had a regular spot at the Saturday morning farmer's market in town. Then I wrote a poem and sent it along with a little bear to some friends who had just learned that their newborn son would never mentally progress beyond infancy.

That little bear was such an encouragement to that one couple, that we contacted a local Christian bookstore about adding a few of what we were calling the "Burden Bear" to their gift offerings. The bears sold well, and a few dozen bears later, I contacted a nationwide gift catalog. That's when things got out of hand—almost.

The woman in charge of selecting product for the gift catalog called me on the phone, expressing an understandable reluctance about taking on something created in a home setting. Her concern was with the issue of supply. I assured her that if the product did well and she needed 100 bears, I could fill the order within ten days. (Mind you: I was buying bears retail at the local Walmart and decorating them with fragments of old quilts I already owned—quilts that were little more than rags.)

Well. The first issue of the gift catalog featuring Burden Bear released, and Diane called me. She needed a *thousand* bears. I'd barely (no pun intended) gotten over the shock when she called again a few days later. She needed *two thousand* bears. I went into high gear locating a wholesale supplier for the bears we'd been buying retail at Walmart. After timing myself to see how long it took me to assemble a Burden Bear, I enlisted the help of other homeschooling moms, who would help me add quilt fragments and bows and poems. I made sure my workers would earn at least minimum wage by paying them per piece. After all, homeschooling moms rarely get uninterrupted hours in which to accomplish anything. Paying them by the piece ensured a fair wage and it didn't matter how often the assembly process got interrupted.

The demand for Burden Bear continued unabated, and an inspirational gift company was born, which we named Prairie Pieceworks. The children were all involved in the day-to-day operation. Our eldest daughter helped with product design. She also learned to run the computer-based accounting program that helped us with billing. Our younger children helped with assembly, packaging, and shipping. We would eventually produce a wholesale catalog featuring plush bears, bunnies, and lambs with poetic messages, handcrafted wood items, and greeting cards featuring my poetry and sporting original design pewter pins. We attended the Christian Booksellers Association international trade show to present our product to Christian bookstore owners.

In a 1993 interview Bob said, "Brooke and Zachary probably know more about business than I did when I was in college. The Lord has blessed us beyond anything we would have ever dreamed of asking. We not only have the privilege of seeing our children learn, but we also have the joy of knowing that what we are creating is meaningful. We can't imagine a more wonderful way for our family to spend its time than in producing gifts that will encourage the faithful in their walk with Christ."

The tagline for our business was "encouraging the faithful." By the time we closed the company in 1994 (because Mom had been contracted to write three novels), our gift products were sold in hundreds of bookstores nationwide. Burden Bear had become the best-selling product ever in the gift catalog. Our family had traveled to Atlanta, Anaheim, and Denver, where the children helped to man our tradeshow booth and enjoyed the sights and sounds of places our family might never have seen were it not for the insanity that was Prairie Pieceworks. And we'd shipped nearly 200,000 bears.

Burden Bear

I'm not a very fancy bear;
    I'm plain and rather small.
Just the same, someone who likes you
    said that I should come to call.
Hide me underneath your pillow
    or set me on a nearby shelf,
And when you feel discouraged,
    I will do my best to help.
I brought my favorite blanket
    that I cuddle when I'm sad—
It's a present from my Granny,
    made for days when things seem bad.
My Granny always told me,
    "Life is like a patchwork quilt—
Just give Jesus all the pieces
    and He'll make a pretty quilt."
Sometimes *I* don't see the pattern,
    sometimes *He* seems far away,
Then I clutch my favorite blanket
    and I pray, and pray, and pray.
Though I don't have all the answers
    (for I'm just a Burden Bear),
I've been sent here on a mission
    from someone who really cares.
When you see me, please remember:
    YOU are in their thoughts and prayers.

Angel Bear

I'm a bear-y special angel
  sent to one who's loved a lot.
When you're lonely and discouraged,
  thinking friends have "just forgot,"
Look at me and know it isn't true—
  we love and pray for you.
May the Lord grant peace and wisdom,
May your gray skies soon be blue.

Wedding Bears

In the hurry of the planning,
    in the rush of all the lists,
Please remember there's a blueprint
    for perfect, wedding bliss.
God designed what we call marriage,
    and He knows how it should work,
    and He wrote down His instructions
    in the book we call His Word.
As you read it, He'll enable you
    to do just what it says,
Then your marriage will be filled
    with heavenly joy and happiness.
We are wishing you His blessings,
    we are praying you will know
    constant blessings sent from heaven
    as you serve Him here below.

Graduation Bear

I've a Ph.D. in honey, so I'm qualified to say
    that I know just how you're feeling
    about Graduation Day.
You can BEAR-ly wait to get there,
    You're excited as can be—
Those were exactly my emotions
    when I got my Ph.D.
As you venture out into the world,
    be faithful to the Lord,
For He can guide and comfort you
    when you obey His Word.
And as you serve and love Him,
    as you seek His will and pray,
You will know the way to true success:
    being faithful every day.

Welcome, Little Lamb

Tiny fingers, tiny toes,
 rosebud mouth and button nose,
Cries that wake you in the night,
 smiles that greet the morning light.
God has sent a tiny treasure,
 showered blessing without measure;
Taken two and made them three,
 formed a brand-new family.
As you raise His little lamb,
 may you know God's perfect plan.
May He bless you with His love,
 send His wisdom from above.

Some-Bunny

Some-bunny loves you,
    yes, some-bunny cares.
When you're tested and tried,
    you are kept in our prayers.
If we can't solve the problem
    or take it away,
We will pray for endurance
    each step of the way.
For the Lord will uphold you
    when your strength is gone,
We are praying you'll know
    that you're never alone.
For some-bunny is praying
    and some-bunny cares.
As you're tested and tried,
    you'll be kept in our prayers.

Friendship Bear

When I was young I hoped to find
    a friend who would be true,
Who would heal my broken spirit,
    who would listen when I'm blue.
Yet, I never knew my future
    would include such a dear friend—
Someone who knew just how to listen
    and on whom I could depend.
Then God heard my need for someone
    and He answered it with *you.*
Thank you, friend, for reaching out
    and now I'm reaching back to you.
With a gift to say I'm grateful
    for the friendship that we share.
She's designed for this occasion,
    for she's called a "Friendship Bear."
And I hope that she'll remind you,
    even when we are apart,
That your friendship is a treasure—
    that I hold you in my heart.

Grandpa Bear

My Grandpa can remember
    When they didn't have TV.
And he walked at least a dozen miles
    To school—when he was three!
He worked all day and night
    To earn a nickel or a dime.
When my Grandpa was a boy,
    He couldn't play—there wasn't time.
But now that Grandpa's grown up
    I can sit upon his knee,
And he tells me lots of stories
    From when he was young, like me.
When my Mom and Dad are busy
    With the things they have to do,
I just go and visit Grandpa—
    We have fun until they're through.
For my Grandpa likes to hug me
    And he laughs at all my jokes.
He reminds me to love Jesus
    And to listen to my folks.
Yes, my Grandpa is the greatest,
    He's a blessing from above.
So I'm giving him this "Grand-BEAR"
    To say, "Grandpa, YOU are loved!"

Teacher Bear

Teachers work so hard at teaching
 that we sometimes quite forget
That they have a home and family
 and needs that must be met.
But we're giving you this gift to say
 we know and that we care—
We appreciate your faithfulness
 and the wisdom that you share.
May God bless you in the classroom,
 may He bless you in the home,
May He comfort, guide, and strengthen you
 wherever you may roam.

Sister Bear

When I need a friend to listen
    or a warrior who will pray,
I can always call my sister—
    she sends help without delay.
For my sister's an example
    of a godly woman's life;
She gives loving help and guidance,
    and she models what is right.
I'm so bear-y, bear-y thankful
    that even when we are apart,
We're not just ordinary sisters—
    we are sisters of the heart.

Birthday Bear

If I could make a perfect bear-thday,
    that's exactly what I'd do.
I'd create a day of blessings,
    then I'd send them on to you.
There'd be honey and a tree to climb,
    a river full of fish—
But on second thought, that's probably not
    exactly what *you'd* wish.
So, I'm asking God to bless you
    in a very special way—
May He give you just what's needed
    for a happy (human) birthday.

Valentine's Bear

Love is patient, love is kind;
    when somehow wronged, love doesn't mind.
Love BEARS all things (I like that part),
    and patience sets true love apart.
While only God loves perfectly,
    His love has flowed through you to me.
I'm grateful for this chance to say
    I love you—Happy Valentine's Day!

Mother Bear

Children seldom thank their mothers
    for the countless things they do—
Hours of cooking and of cleaning,
    ready hugs when kids feel blue.
But today I want to tell you
    that I often thank the Lord
That He blessed me with a Mother
    who depends upon the Lord.
You've been faithful in your service
    both to God and family.
Thank you, Mom, for your example,
    thanks for all you've done for me.

Grandma Bear

I'm a "Granny Bear" sent 'specially
by one of your "grand-cubs"
Who gives thanks to God the Father
for your special kind of love.
Thank you for your time and laughter,
thank you also for your prayers.
Thanks for sharing all the wisdom
God has taught you through the years.
May you know that you are treasured
by the ones whose hands you hold.
May the Lord grant joy and laughter
in the future that unfolds.

Garden Bear

The Christian life and gardening
    have lots of things they share—
And here's a small reminder
    from a friendly Garden Bear:
To grow in grace and knowledge,
    to reflect the One we serve,
We must daily weed our hearts and minds
    by taking in His Word.
Once our gardens have been weeded,
    we can plant some seeds of faith,
Watching daily for the harvest,
    learning patiently to wait.
So remember when you garden
    and you tire of all the work:
Eternal lessons can be learned
    while digging in the dirt.

Hope at Easter

Hope knows there isn't anything
    that's stronger than God's love.
Hope promises eternal life
    in mansions up above.
Hope means we realize the truth
    in every Bible verse.
Hope reassures when life just seems
    to go from bad to worse.
Hope knows that caterpillars
    do emerge as butterflies.
Hope knows the sun is waiting
    just beyond the blackest skies.
Hope lives beyond Good Friday
    to that resurrection morn
When the Lord of hope and glory
    won the way to be reborn.
As you celebrate this Easter
    May your hopes and dreams come true,
May you know the lasting presence
    of the One who died for you.

Noel

If I could have you over
    for a cup of Christmas tea,
I would pray for just a chance to share
    what Christmas means to me.
It's more than just the story
    of a special baby's birth
And it's more than just the news
    that someone great once walked the earth.
For the baby in the manger
    grew to manhood just to die
For the sins of every human—
    and that means for you and I.
So, while Christmas is the birthday
    of a special baby boy,
Please remember: Christ as *Savior*
    is the Source of lasting joy.

Books: The Stories Behind the Stories

It is good to give thanks to the LORD
And to sing praises to Your name, O Most High
… To declare Your lovingkindness in the morning
And Your faithfulness by night.
Psalm 92:1-2 NASB

I did not plan to become a novelist. I never dreamed of seeing my name on a book cover. Then again, I never planned to get married (but I have—twice), never planned to have children (four and a beloved stepson), never planned to homeschool (all four), and certainly never planned to marry again after being widowed in 2001 (2003). I often say that my life is proof God has a sense of humor and that I'm never saying *never* again.

My road to publication was atypical. The story that would become *Walks the Fire* resulted from my teaching Nebraska history to my four homeschooled children. We had moved to an acreage, and the fourth-grade curriculum included the history of Nebraska. Since I didn't grow up in Nebraska, I was learning along with the children.

When it became obvious that my children were bored with the textbook (imagine that), I decided that we'd walk down to the abandoned pioneer cemetery between us and the main road and begin to learn about the people buried there. I asked questions. How many of these trees were here when Mrs. King died? (None.) What did these people do when their children were sick? (There wasn't a doctor in town, and the row of graves for five children of the same parents provided a sobering answer to that question. When I told my four that only one of them would have survived without penicillin, they began to realize that *history* was about *real people.*) As we began to learn about the people represented by dates and timelines, my children's attitude about history changed. They may be the only ones in the state who made scrapbooks based on a cemetery. And it was their idea!

At some point in the process of teaching my children about Nebraska history, I became fascinated with the lives of the pioneer women who'd settled the state. How would I have felt living in a sod house instead of a log cabin? What would it have been like to leave my parents and siblings behind, knowing I might never see them again? The questions mounted up, and I went looking for answers in published diaries and memoirs. I began playing with an imaginary woman named Jesse King. She was part of the first wagon train to cross Nebraska that included families. It was 1843, and Jesse didn't want to go west.

Jesse became real to me, and I wanted to finish her story. But there was a problem. I didn't have time to write seriously.

Part of our homeschooling included developing a home-based business. The first business revolved around growing organic produce and maintaining a regular stand at the Saturday morning farmers market in town. We eventually added craft items to our offerings, and one of those items birthed an inspirational gift company. Prairie Pieceworks grew rapidly. The children were involved in product design, bookkeeping, production, and shipping. We had product not only in catalogs but also in hundreds of Christian bookstores across the nation. I couldn't possibly keep up with Prairie Pieceworks and write a novel.

I'd published a couple of things in magazines, and I knew what happened to people who dreamed of getting a book published. Rejection. And so, expecting rejection—which would give me permission to put my story away and finish it one day for my grandchildren—I accessed the 1993 edition of the *Writer's Market* at the public library and wrote three query letters.

Weeks went by, and then I got a request for sample chapters from one of the publishers—the only one to respond to my query letter. I sent sample chapters. More time went by, and I was equally thrilled and horrified to receive a request for the whole book. I didn't have a whole book. Panicked, I called a friend who had published many magazine articles and asked her what to do. She advised me to tell them I'd send them the novel in X weeks—however long I thought it would take me to finish the book. That's what I did.

The time came and went for me to send the promised manuscript off, and that darned gift company had been so busy I hadn't been able to finish the book. But I knew they would reject it anyway, so I sent what I had—which was about two-thirds of the novel, including the more dramatic scenes and the ending. I inserted space-holders along the way. "This chapter hasn't been written yet—here's what happens." I really didn't give it much thought. They were going to reject it anyway, and I was busy with homeschooling and running the home-based business.

As you know by now, Thomas Nelson Publishers didn't reject the book. Bob and I came home one evening to a message (landline with answering machine).

"Stephanie, this is Lonnie Hull Dupont with Thomas Nelson Publishers." She wanted me to call her back! They were making an offer they hoped I wouldn't refuse (she actually said exactly that).

When the contract arrived, it wasn't just for one book. It was for three—because, after all, series were "the thing" in historical fiction. I remember looking at my husband and saying, "I don't know if I can write three books. I haven't even written one yet." My practical husband responded, "They're paying you money. Sign the contract."

And that's how I became published. Re-telling it only makes me marvel anew at how God worked, because that wasn't a stroke of luck. God was at work providing for me and the kids. In a few years, He'd be taking Bob home to heaven. After years as a full-time homemaker, I had no marketable skills. But by the time Bob graduated to heaven in 2001, I had enough books in the marketplace that along with widows' benefits and life insurance and some very careful budgeting, I would be able to meet our goal, which was to remain in the home until my youngest graduated high school. That's all I wanted, and God provided it. He's still providing, all these years later. And I'm still in awe.

1995 ***Walks the Fire,***
Book 1, Prairie Winds Series
Find it here: https://tinyurl.com/y35htbuz

1996 ***Soaring Eagle,*** Book 2,
Prairie Winds Series
Find it here: https://tinyurl.com/y2e2rc8g

Finding a happy ending for a nineteenth century Lakota man is not an easy task. Soaring Eagle's character was inspired by Dr. Charles Eastman (Ohiyesa), a Santee Sioux physician educated at Dartmouth College and Boston University. To research the Lakota, I read dozens of books on the history and culture, doing my best to find accounts written by men and women who had experienced the events in my novel—books like *The Middle Five* by Francis La Flesche and *Land of the Spotted Eagle* by Standing Bear. While browsing the biography section at the public library one day, I was drawn to an old book on the shelf. Without reading the spine, I pulled it down. I was holding a copy of *Mary and I: Forty Years with the Sioux* by Dr. Stephen Return Riggs. The Riggses' son, Alfred, was headmaster at the Santee Normal Training School in Santee, Nebraska. This was where I sent Soaring Eagle in my novel. Books like *Blue Star* by Duncan illuminated the missionary experience and helped create Carrie Brown (Red Bird).

1997 ***Red Bird***, Book 3,
Prairie Winds Series
Find it here: https://tinyurl.com/y6ox3lcf

As often happens in my writing, a minor character walks on stage and grabs more of the limelight than I had intended giving them. Such was the case with Sarah Biddle, who ran away from an orphan train in the closing chapters of *Walks the Fire*. As her story unfolded, I decided that Sarah deserved a happily ever after, and so I proposed that she be the main character in Book 1 of my second series, Keepsake Legacies.

This series of books departed from the format of my first series, in that the three books do not feature chronological events featuring the same characters. While I do recommend that people read the Prairie Winds series in order, that isn't necessary with Keepsake Legacies, because each of those stories is intended to be a stand-alone. The reason they are connected in a series has to do with the story hook. Each story shows the connection between the main character and a keepsake that was important to her. For Sarah of *Sarah's Patchwork*, the important keepsake is a crazy quilt, and each of the book's chapters is titled for a fabric in Sarah's quilt. Events in each chapter show why Sarah kept a certain scrap of fabric and used it in her quilt. In *Karyn's Memory Box*, each chapter is titled for a small keepsake that an elderly woman cherished and kept in a small box that moved with her as aging required that she downsize. *Nora's Ribbon of Memories* is a charm string of antique buttons, with each button representing something special to Nora, a dressmaker/milliner.

1998 ***Sarah's Patchwork***,
Book 1, Keepsake Legacies Series
Find it here: https://tinyurl.com/y6pkg97u

1999 ***Karyn's Memory Box***,
Book 2, Keepsake Legacies Series
Find it here: https://tinyurl.com/y5y4u38u

1999 ***Nora's Ribbon of Memories***,
Book 3, Keepsake Legacies Series
Find it here: https://tinyurl.com/yxo7qttu

My next series, titled Dakota Moons, resulted from research I did for the book *Soaring Eagle*. While seeking a happy ending for Soaring Eagle, I became aware of the event that we now call the Dakota War of 1862. (Back when I was researching, it was called the Dakota Sioux Uprising.) I was profoundly moved by the heroism of some of the Christian Dakota Sioux swept up in events not of their making. My desire to pay tribute to those brave men and women resulted in this series—my second three-book series that really should be read in order.

2000 ***Valley of the Shadow***,
Book 1, Dakota Moons Series
Find it here: https://tinyurl.com/yy7kypde
Finalist for the Christy Award

2001 ***Edge of the Wilderness***,
Book 2, Dakota Moons Series
Find it here: https://tinyurl.com/yykjltbc
Finalist for the Christy Award

2002 ***Heart of the Sandhills***,
Book 3, Dakota Moons Series
Find it here: https://tinyurl.com/y33vb2p6

Researching my first seven novels set in Nebraska took me to the Nebraska Sandhills and Fort Robinson. Firm in my conviction that I'd never want to set a book later than 1900, I was convinced otherwise when I learned about the German prisoners of war who did harvesting and ranch work in various parts of the United States during WWII.

Then, there was a bit of a hiccup on the business side of things.

Writers who remain in the traditional publishing industry for long inevitably learn that the only thing that's certain about a writing life is that nothing is certain. Since my leap into the industry in 1994, I've experienced the hiring, firing, and transferring of editors I loved—and some I didn't love quite so much. Some publishers have promoted my work "to the ends of the earth" and others barely acknowledged I was their author. One of the biggest changes I encountered early on in my writing career came in 2001, the year my husband died. My publisher was going through a time of change and wasn't sure about including historical fiction (my genre) in production plans. I remain thankful that said publisher understood my situation. I didn't have the luxury of waiting while they decided what they were going to do about historical fiction. As a result, Thomas Nelson freed me from contractual obligations. Subsequently, my agent won me a place with Bethany House Publishers. I felt like a gold star had been pinned on my lapel. Many of the authors I most admired wrote for Bethany House.

2003 ***Secrets on the Wind,***
Book 1, Pine Ridge Portraits
Find it here: https://tinyurl.com/y4o4eowb

2004 ***Watchers on the Hill***,
Book 2, Pine Ridge Portraits
Find it here: https://tinyurl.com/yxf4dkhc

2005 ***Footprints on the Horizon***,
Book 3, Pine Ridge Portraits
Find it here: https://tinyurl.com/y3zx3y5j

After the publication of my ninth historical fiction novel, my career took another detour, this time into contemporary fiction. In February of 2001, my husband of twenty-seven years died of non-Hodgkins lymphoma. Our children were ages 11, 15, 18, and 20. That Christmas, a niece who was living in Geneva, Switzerland, invited us to spend the holidays with her. While running away from home and avoiding the first Christmas without Bob sounded like a great idea, I didn't think it would be financially possible. As it turned out, it was. Because of the horrific events of September 1 that year, airfares were low. With the encouragement of my financial advisor, I planned the trip, never suspecting it would inspire not one but two novels.

I'd fallen in love with all things French as a high school French student. I majored in French in college and spent a magical summer attending school in a small town in southern France. My children didn't know the part of me that spoke French. I hadn't met Bob when I went to school in Arcachon. Hence, he wasn't part of my French memories. That made the trip especially healing for me, as it carried me back to a time when I'd been incredibly happy. An author friend cheered me on about that trip, and when I wrote her about our time in France, she wrote back, "When am I going to read this novel?" I replied that I didn't write contemporary fiction. But Lois Gladys Leppard (author of the beloved Mandie series of young adult books) would not let it go. She harangued me until I began to think about a possible storyline. The result was my next two novels.

2005 ***A Garden in Paris***
Find it here: https://tinyurl.com/yxuvvue9

2006 ***A Hilltop in Tuscany*** (sequel to *A Garden in Paris*)
Find it here: https://tinyurl.com/y38nbv5w

2005 ***How to Help a Grieving Friend: A Candid Guide for Those Who Care*** (nonfiction)
Find it here: https://tinyurl.com/y2v9dkw6

When my husband died in 2001, our church experienced the loss of two other very involved members. Both of them, like Bob, were parents of young children. Those of us who were left behind comforted one another as best we could. We all learned a lot, not only about how *not* to comfort others but also how it should be done. More than once, I called the widowed husband of my best friend who had passed away five years earlier to apologize for something I'd done or said when Celest died. I'd been well meaning but clueless. Now that I was in Dan's shoes, I realized that some of the things I'd said intending to encourage him not only didn't encourage but probably hurt him. He was gracious to forgive. Eventually, I began to wish for a way to share what I'd learned—a way to help others avoid being well-meaning but clueless.

My brother, a funeral director for all of his professional life, agreed there was a need for the kind of book I eventually began to plan. He was a great encouragement. After a few meetings with the other young widows and widowers I knew, I began to write. I spoke with my agent about a book. With her encouragement I developed a manuscript that she began to market to nonfiction publishers. It was slow going. She often heard, "We don't do death and dying well." She always replied, "And that's exactly why this book is needed," and she eventually found the book a home with NavPress. My editor and I devised a format that organized the material around two topics: first, *how it feels* to be the one grieving, and second, *how to help.* The goal was to provide an easy-to-read tool for anyone wondering what to say and what to do to help others. It's an honor to have my name on the cover.

2007 ***Jacob's List***

Find it here: https://tinyurl.com/y37ow3vd

Bethany House wasn't sure it was a good idea to let me move into the world of contemporary fiction, but when I proposed *A Garden in Paris*, they believed in the story and asked for a sequel. Perhaps I would increase my reading audience by segueing into a genre that had more readers than did historical fiction at the time. We were very, very, wrong. Sales were poor, and for a while I thought my career might be over. Thankfully, God thought otherwise.

I was at the Nebraska State Historical Society Archives doing research for a quilt history book (see below for the nonfiction title that came out in 2012) one day, when one of the researchers drew me aside. "You'd love learning about a Nebraska gal I just pulled records on." Someone writing about long distance horseback rides had inquired about Nan Aspinwall, a Nebraska gal Buffalo Bill Cody challenged, betting her that she couldn't do a solo horseback ride from San Francisco to New York. Nan won that bet. I was intrigued. "What do we have of hers?" The researcher smiled. "We have her scrapbooks."

I returned to the archive the following Monday, paged through Nan's scrapbooks, and called my agent with a new idea for a novel that would take me back to my first love, historical fiction. My agent made a phone call. Bethany House said yes to the book. They wanted it instead of the contemporary book I was writing. Could I manage the required research and still meet my deadline? I didn't hesitate to promise *yes*. I kept that promise, but it wasn't easy. My family ate a lot of carry-out while I was buried in research and writing.

2008 **Belle of the Wild West** (originally published as *Unbridled Dreams*)
Find it here: https://tinyurl.com/y2k6qf75

It has long been my habit to continually read "real history," both because I want to learn about a given topic of interest and because I never know when something will tweak my curiosity. When I ask myself *what would that have been like*, I know I should keep researching. When I begin to ask *what if,* I'm usually on to the setting for a novel. A blurry black-and-white photograph of Madame Canutson of South Dakota (a female bullwhacker) and equally blurry black-and-white photographs of women standing near sluices wedged into the canyons above Deadwood during the Gold Rush resulted in my 2009 book about a woman gold miner and her friend, a female bullwhacker.

2009 ***A Claim of Her Own***
Find it here: https://tinyurl.com/y4pcszsu

2010 ***Sixteen Brides***
Find it here: https://tinyurl.com/y2bdznvf

The journey that brought me to writing fiction began with wondering about the women who came west. That interest has never wavered, and over the years I've encountered unforgettable stories of single women who took advantage of the Homestead Act of 1862 and made homes for themselves. Those women inspired *Sixteen Brides*, in which five determined women duped by a dishonest land agent join forces. I wanted to call the book *Sixteen Widows*, because the sixteen women in my group of emigrants are all Civil War widows. Thankfully, Bethany House convinced me to opt for a happier title.

I had been happily remarried for about seven years when I talked my second husband into joining me as a student at Nebraska Wesleyan University in Lincoln, Nebraska, where we'd work on a Master of Historical Studies degree. The program was a hybrid program designed for public school history and social studies teachers, and because of the target audience, it focused on North American history. I begged our way into the program and loved nearly every minute of the two years we worked on our degrees (awarded in 2012). During our time with that program, we visited DeSoto National Wildlife Refuge where the cargo of the steamboat Bertrand, which sank in 1865, was on display. I saw fabric swatches and other artifacts, among them possessions of three young women en route to Montana, where their parents had opened a dry goods store, serving people swarming into the area because of yet another gold rush. The steamboat itself and the river journey captured my imagination and provided inspiration for my next novel.

2011 ***A Most Unsuitable Match***
Find it here: https://tinyurl.com/y243km7n

Research for this novel would result in my being fascinated by the era of steamboat travel. I'd "meet" Minnie Hill, one of the first licensed steamboat pilots in America, and while Minnie didn't figure in this novel, she would inspire the main character in a novel yet-to-come. (See below.)

2011 ***Home on the Plains: Quilts and the Sod House Experience*** (nonfiction)
Find it here: https://tinyurl.com/y2eey8uc

Another bump in my career path took me from Bethany House to Barbour in 2011. At last I was able to convince someone to let me tell quilt stories. I've been an avid quilt lover since first gathering with a quilting group in the late 1980s to finish a quilt I'd begun but never finished as a wedding gift for a dear friend. I grew up around the craft, as my mother spent hours embroidering quilt blocks that she'd set into quilt tops and quilt. She made quilts for each of her children and many of her grandchildren. But when I first tried making my own quilt in the early 1970s, I hated everything about the process. I gritted my teeth and finished that first quilt all the way to the edge, and then I folded it up and put it away—that was that. But by the late 1980s, I felt differently. The women who offered to help me finish that project became dear friends. Our children crawled beneath the quilting frame while we talked and laughed—and sometimes cried over problems and trials. Quilting became more about the women doing it than the object in the quilting frame. I had a new passion. Old quilts.

I took classes on dating textiles, joined the local quilt guild, and discovered a world where there was always something new to learn. But it wasn't necessarily about the quilt itself. More often than not for me personally, it was about the woman who'd created it. Why did she use that screaming yellow fabric? Where was she when she pieced these blocks? What secret hurt did making this quilt help to heal? Why didn't she ever finish this lovely little crib quilt? Is this stain a remnant of a home remedy—and if it is, did it work? I wanted to tell quilt stories.

Barbour Publishing gave me the opportunity to do that. The three-book series I wrote for Barbour is a series only because each book tells the rest of the story behind a certain type of antique quilt. The characters and situations are unique to each book.

2012 ***The Key on the Quilt***
Find it here: https://tinyurl.com/y4cmlfhm
Inspired by the story of a prison warden's wife who single-handedly quelled a riot in 1875.

2012 ***The Shadow on the Quilt***
Find it here: https://tinyurl.com/yyxudtrd

Winner of Romantic Times Magazine's Reviewers' Choice Award for Best Inspiration Romance of 2012

Inspired by the women of Lincoln, Nebraska, who created the Home for the Friendless, which served the homeless, the poor, and unwed mothers in the late nineteenth century. I became aware of the Home for the Friendless when I inquired about a small "H. of F." sign at Wyuka Cemetery in Lincoln, near where my husband, Bob, was laid to rest.

2012 "**A Patchwork Love**," novella in the collection titled ***A Patchwork Christmas***
Find it here: https://tinyurl.com/yycupxlo

One of the blessings of writing is meeting kindred spirits and sisters in Christ. Judith Miller and Nancy Moser have been both for many years. We've written several Christmas anthologies together. *A Patchwork Christmas* was the first. My novella in this collection is based on a real event told by a Nebraska pioneer in a collection of sod house memories—stories told by people who'd lived in those iconic soddies on the Nebraska prairie.

2013 ***The Message on the Quilt***
Find it here: https://tinyurl.com/y3p8mdfr

Inspired by the educational movement known as the Chautauqua Movement and set at the 1890 Chautauqua that took place in Beatrice, Nebraska. The Chautauqua Movement began in New York. It was an early attempt to make education available to the masses. Home studies were developed and certificates awarded to those who completed various programs. The meetings attracted thousands to hear well-known lecturers and to attend musical and cultural events over the course of a week or ten days.

2014 ***A Captain for Laura Rose***
Find it here: https://tinyurl.com/y6bod89a

Steamboat pilot Minnie Hill (whom I learned about while researching *A Most Unsuitable Match)* inspired my return to the days of steamboat travel on the treacherous Missouri River.

2015 ***Daughter of the Regiment***
Find it here: https://tinyurl.com/y45eshrz

I never intended to tell a Civil War story. First, because I've tended to focus on the Great Plains as a setting, and second, because the subject is so vast and so fraught with emotion that it intimidates me. Two museum encounters overcame my reluctance. First, I heeded a highway sign on Interstate 70 in Missouri indicating the presence of a Confederate cemetery. I'd seen it countless times, making the journey from southeast Nebraska to southern Illinois where my family lived. But I hadn't *seen* it. When I finally heeded that sign and visited not only the cemetery but also the Oliver Anderson house near Lexington, Missouri, I was astounded. Plantations? In *Missouri*? I had no idea. I began to learn. When the Museum of Missouri History in St. Louis mounted an exhibition about Missouri in the Civil War, I attended. The exhibit introduced me to the role of women in the war. Somewhere along the way, I became aware of Daughters of the Regiment. There was my story, narrowed down to a setting I felt I could manage—the Battle of Lexington, Missouri—and populated by women I could research.

2015 "**A Stitch in Time**," novella in the collection titled ***A Basket Brigade Christmas***
Find it here: https://tinyurl.com/yy8er4rw

Another museum visit, this one to the Illinois history museum in Springfield to view an exhibit about Illinois in the Civil War, inspired this collection of stories. The exhibit illuminated the contributions women made to the war effort. I was showing my photographs of the exhibit to a friend, and when she read one of the quotes on display at the museum, she laughed and said, "I want to read this story." Here's the original quote (an actual note accompanying an aid society shipment) that inspired this idea:

> "My dear boy, I have knit these socks expressly for you. How do you like them? How do you look, and where do you live when you are at home? I am of medium height, of slight build, with blue eyes, fair complexion, light hair, and a good deal of it. Write and tell me all about yourself and how you get on in the hospitals. P.S. If the recipient of these socks has a wife will he please exchange socks with some poor fellow not so fortunate."

I had fun imagining "the rest of the story."

2016 ***Messenger by Moonlight***
Find it here: https://tinyurl.com/y635mhgc

The Civil War played a central role in the creation of the Pony Express. As war loomed, Washington was concerned about how ties would be maintained between the Union and the western states. Communication would be critical, and the main mail route to the West would be shut off if the Southern states seceded, because it went through states that would be loyal to the South. At a meeting with one senator, Alexander Majors promised to create an alternative that would deliver mail from Missouri (where the telegraph ended) all the way to Sacramento in ten days. That incredible feat birthed the Pony Express. Of course *I* wanted to know about the women at the Pony Express stations—the ones who fed the riders and station keepers. That was a quest that would involve reading between the lines, because the women involved in the effort are barely mentioned. I did my best.

2018 "**Mending Hearts**," a novella in the collection titled ***Christmas Stitches***
Find it here: https://tinyurl.com/y5z3oezv

This story was intended to be a full-length novel set in a Mennonite community in Pennsylvania. I first became aware of this unique group when volunteering as a docent for a quilt exhibit at the International Quilt Study Center and Museum in my home town. This particular group of Mennonites dressed like all their Victorian counterparts—until they joined the church, at which time they began to dress in the simple manner most connected with Old Order Mennonites. What precipitated that unique practice fascinated me and suggested a novel. But I am not known for stories set among the Mennonite community, and I eventually decided that I couldn't do it justice. Thus, "Mending Hearts" became a typical Stephanie Whitson novella, set in small town nineteenth century Nebraska. With quilting.

2019 ***Love at First Light***

My first foray into the world of indie publishing, this novel has long been on my heart. As I compile this list for those interested in reading my books in order, I'm deep into the lives of Isobel Manning and Gideon Long, doing my best to tell a story that, while being true to history, will also have a happy ending. I believe in happy endings.

Tributes

*The lines are fallen unto me in pleas-
ant places; yea, I have a goodly heritage.*
Psalm 16:6 KJV

Farewell

October 4, 1989

As an emotional adolescent I watched Secretariat run his last race on TV. Far removed from the horse-racing world and yet caught up in the saga of a great thoroughbred's career, I cried. Tears streamed as I saw him thunder down the stretch with that great, bounding stride. I felt sure I would never see such a horse again, and my love for horses—specifically for *that* horse—swelled my heart.

It was not until I was married that I found a kindred spirit in my love for Big Red. My husband and I read the books about him together. For our most memorable anniversary celebration, he surprised me with the film *Secretariat's Last Race*. He had made many long-distance phone calls to locate it and have it mailed from the state of New York. It was a gift of love and we enjoyed that film as much as any replay of *Gone with the Wind*.

We had been married twelve years and had two children when a vacation trip to the East brought another surprise and dream come true. Bob called

Claiborne Farms and, unbeknownst to me, arranged for us to visit Big Red. Watching Secretariat race across his paddock toward us literally took my breath away. Here he was, in the flesh, and I was actually touching, petting, feeding the Great One peppermint candy. It was a moment to cherish, and one I've never forgotten. Our tour escort must have sensed my deep joy, for he pulled some red hairs from Red's curry comb and gave them to me. Others might laugh at my childish happiness, but I didn't care. I still have Secretariat's tail-feathers—and 11x14 photos of him racing across his paddock adorn our living room wall.

And so I sat at the supper table tonight and wept like a child whose puppy had died, when my husband shared today's sad news.

I am one of those born-again Christians who subscribes to a literal interpretation of the Bible. In Revelation there is a reference to the armies of heaven being astride white horses. I expect to be among that army of riders, and if heaven is really a place where all our wishes come true, I know one thing for certain: I may ride a white horse in God's army, but when the war is over, I'll ask to make a trade. And then my horse will be Red.

My Dad

Cecil Grayson Irvin graduated to heaven in 1996. I wrote this tribute as a Father's Day gift to him in about 1983. Just before he died, he promised to meet me just inside the gate. The older I get, the more I look forward to that day. I know he'll be there. Daddy was a man of honor. He always kept his word.

My dad is a tall, slender man ("Slim" the guys at work used to call him) with gentle blue eyes and slightly rounded shoulder caused, I am sure, by years of bending his 6'5" frame to catch the words of those shorter than he.

Of course I can't remember it, but the family tells of Dad teaching me to walk by standing me on the toes of his shoes as he walked backwards.

I remember as a child waiting excitedly for the car to pull up in the drive when he returned from his over-the-road trucking job. He would unfold his tall frame from the driver's seat and put on the brown cap that matched his driver's uniform. Dad took pride in his well-pressed uniforms with the company badge embroidered on the shoulder. We often laughed to see other motorists slow noticeably when we passed, thinking they were being monitored by a policeman in an unmarked car.

When I was little, he was often on the road. But when he was home, I climbed onto his lap after meals, just for the feeling of being sheltered by his arms while he visited with Mother or read the evening paper. When I grew older—with Tuesday and Thursday Dad's nights home—Mother would cook cornbread with ham and beans or round steak with biscuits, and we would bask in his presence, just glad that he would be there to share our supper, coffee, and late night popcorn.

On Sundays Dad read me the comics and then entertained me by taking out pen and paper and drawing Dick Tracy and Brenda Starr. I still love to read the comic strips, enduring considerable chiding from my husband for the habit. I can't copy the characters as Dad did, but I occasionally clip one to slip into Bob's lunch sack. He enjoys it, in spite of himself.

When childhood terrors over starting school after the summer overtook me, Dad was there to help relax the wrenching knot in my stomach. With his quiet voice he reassured me that everything would be all right. I believed him, and the knot loosened, and it *was* all right.

I don't remember his ever spanking me. Mother says he didn't. He never had to. There was just something in his quiet love for me that motivated me to obey.

In the days before seat belts and car seats, Dad used to sit me on his lap and let me think I was guiding the car.

On summer nights when I was in junior high, we went to baseball games, sitting high in stadium seats provided by the St. Louis Cardinals to students with the right grade point average. Dad bought me soda pop and peanuts, and we cheered Orlando Cepeda, Bob Gibson, and Lou Brock. I knew every player's batting average and skipped classes once to watch the World Series on TV. Without Dad in the next seat, baseball just isn't much fun anymore.

He taught me to drive defensively—and then trusted me with his car on a weekend away with other students. I would have done anything to keep from betraying his trust, and we all drove carefully that weekend. Dad must have spent a couple of sleepless nights wondering if his daughter would become another highway statistic. But he trusted me. He understood my need for independence.

I remember my first car. Dad drove it home, parked it in the driveway, and ordered me to change an imaginary flat tire.

He spoiled me. On snowy mornings I would go outside to find my car cleaned off, the driveway shoveled so that I could drive off to classes at the university.

I remember tears in his eyes as he walked me down the aisle to become Mrs. Robert Whitson. Those tears still shine every time we have to say goodbye after a visit that spans the miles between Nebraska and Illinois.

When my first child was born, the familiar knots returned to my stomach over the responsibility of motherhood. Dad reassured me. He drove me to the grocery store and patiently experimented until he found a way to fit the infant seat securely in a grocery cart while still leaving room for groceries. He couldn't have known how much it meant to have him there, his frame towering over me, protecting his "little girl"—and a new granddaughter.

Dad loves the Lord. He serves in quiet ways that people often don't notice. For years he and mother visited widows of fellow drivers killed on the road, providing help with business details, organizing a fund to provide cash in the early days of widowhood. He still chauffeurs "the elderly" around town and on trips to the airport.

Dad taught me how to walk. He taught me to love baseball and comic strip characters and molasses-and-butter on bread. He taught me to obey authority. He proved that things would be all right next year in school, and that I could be an efficient mother, after all. He taught me about my heavenly Father, too. Oh, not with many words, but by being there, by loving, by listening—by being so very much like Him.

I'm over thirty now, and much too old to call my father "Daddy," but he will always be "Daddy" in my heart... in my thoughts... in my prayers... because part of me will always be a little girl when he's around.

Mother

The last time I saw my mother, she didn't know who I was. And yet, I can smile through my tears at the memory of the little old white-haired lady sitting on her bed at the nursing home waving goodbye to me when I turned to look back before stepping into the hall. She was happy. At peace. She knew I was someone nice, and she seemed pleased that I had come to visit. I managed to control the tears until I got to the car in the parking lot, and then I lost it.

My mother—and it was Mother, never "Mom," which she proclaimed disrespectful—was not an easy woman. She bore scars I didn't know about until I had grown up and left home—scars from an unspeakably difficult childhood endured in the days when abuse was hidden and mental illness was something to be ashamed of. You didn't seek help. You just made do. You did the best you could and sometimes the best you could do was to cling to the fringe of sanity while your panicked family called for the pastor to come.

In honor of Mother's Day, I sing her praises, because, in spite of the deep wounds and the regrettable moments and the profound sadness she carried with her, my mother was amazing. She and Daddy were married for nearly sixty years. They modeled commitment, and one thing I know beyond a shadow of a doubt is that I was loved. What a gift.

Mother loved Jesus. Most of the Bible verses I can recite were learned when Mother was the head of the Primary Department or Vacation Bible School or Girl's Auxiliary. Most of the hymns I can sing from memory resonate from a childhood spent sitting next to Mother on a hard pew at a poor Baptist church. We were there for every service. Sunday School and morning church. Training Union and evening church. Wednesday night, too. If the doors were open, we were there. It's a rich heritage.

Mother loved flowers. To this day I sometimes amaze my husband because I know the name of this blooming bush or that tree or those perennials. "That's a flowering quince," I said just last week. "Mother loved them because of those bright blossoms right next to the stem." I don't know if she had a favorite flower, but irises probably ranked right up there. We had several varieties, and I still remember *Wabash*, with its dark blue drops and white crown.

Mother was not a good cook, mostly because she grew up very poor and had to learn to make do. *It's food. Eat it and be thankful.* But she could make a blackberry cobbler like no other, and she always made one for me when I was home to visit. And the fudge she made—only at Christmas—oh, my. Still makes my mouth water to think of it.

She loved books. One of my earliest memories of Mother is of her reading aloud to me when I was sick. *Pinocchio*, I think it was. And while I may doubt the name of the book, I don't doubt that one of the reasons I love words is Mother, who was never allowed to go beyond the 8th grade, found a way to educate herself by reading. She passed on the joy of words to me.

And so, on Mother's Day, I remember Mother and look forward to the day when I'll see her again. She graduated to heaven in 1996. Since then, she's been joined by Daddy, my first husband, the grandson I never met, and an entire host of extended family.

Thank you, Father, for the blessing of Mother.

Books by Stephanie Grace Whitson

Historical Fiction:

Christmas Stitches (novella anthology)
A Basket Brigade Christmas (novella anthology)
A Patchwork Christmas (novella anthology)
Messenger by Moonlight
Daughter of the Regiment
A Captain for Laura Rose

The Quilt Chronicles Series (3 books)
The Message on the Quilt
The Shadow on the Quilt
The Key on the Quilt

Stand-alone books (not part of a series):
A Most Unsuitable Match
Sixteen Brides
A Claim of Her Own
Unbridled Dreams

Pine Ridge Portraits Series (3 books)
Secrets on the Wind, Watchers on the Hill, and Footprints on the Horizon

Dakota Moons Series (3 books)
Valley of the Shadow, Edge of the Wilderness and Heart of the Sandhills

Keepsake Legacies Series (3 books)
Sarah's Patchwork, Karyn's Memory Box, and Nora's Ribbon of Memories

Prairie Winds Series (3 books)
Walks the Fire, Soaring Eagle, and Red Bird

Contemporary Fiction *(3 books)*
Jacob's List, A Garden in Paris, and A Hilltop in Tuscany

Non-Fiction
How to Help a Grieving Friend: A Candid Guide for those who Care
Home on the Plains: Quilts and the Sod House Experience

About Stephanie

Award-winning novelist Stephanie Grace Whitson began playing with imaginary friends (i.e., writing fiction) in the 1990s when an abandoned pioneer cemetery near the Whitsons' country home in Otoe County, Nebraska, provided not only a hands-on history lesson for her four home schooled children, but also a topic of personal study. Her first novel was published in 1995. A lifelong learner, Stephanie earned her master's degree in history from Nebraska Wesleyan University in 2012. As a historian and quilt lover, she has owned a pattern design company, studied textile dating and quilt history with a variety of well-known quilt historians, and taken a series of appraisal classes from the American Quilters Society. She is a member of the American Quilt Study Group and the International Quilt Study Center and Museum and is a regular volunteer at the museum, where she helps with exhibitions, quilt research, and Quilt ID days. Stephanie has developed a series of programs on various historical and spiritual topics and is a frequent speaker at quilt guilds, libraries, and church women's events. When not writing or researching, she enjoys reading, quilting, spoiling her eleven grandchildren and/or Kona Kai (the golden retriever), and riding her motorcycle named Kitty.

Learn more at www.stephaniewhitson.com.

Join the conversation https://www.facebook.com/StephanieGraceWhitsonofficial/

Made in United States
North Haven, CT
08 August 2022

22437174R00088